# THE LITTLE BOOK OF CU T



**MEG AVENT**

# THE LITTLE BOOK OF CUPCAKE TIPS

MEG AVENT

A.
Absolute Press

First published in Great Britain in 2010 by
**Absolute Press**
Scarborough House, 29 James Street West
Bath BA1 2BT, England
**Phone** 44 (0) 1225 316013 **Fax** 44 (0) 1225 445836
**E-mail** info@absolutepress.co.uk
**Web** www.absolutepress.co.uk



A catalogue record of this book is available from the British Library

**ISBN 13: 9781906650438**

Printed and bound in Malta on behalf of Latitude Press

'When you look at a cupcake,
you've got to smile.'

**Anne Byrn,**
**American writer and cook**

# 1

**Never be tempted**

to open the oven door during the first 10 minutes of baking – your

**cupcakes won't rise!**

# 2

Buy a disposable cardboard cupcake stand

**for an impressive, but inexpensive display** for a party.

# 3

# For a delectable packed lunch treat,

slice your un-iced cupcake in half and fill with frosting – this way it won't get ruined in the box!

# 4

A couple of simple ways to

**check your cupcakes have baked – press lightly**

in the middle and it should spring back,

**or push a toothpick in**

and it should come out clean.

# 5

Unless you have a willing helper,

**use a vase or jug to hold your piping bag**

open while you fill it.

# 6

**To help them keep their shape,** leave your cupcakes to cool in their baking tray for 5 minutes after they come out of the oven. No longer or they will have soggy bottoms!

# 7

Cupcakes

# are best eaten on the day

they are baked or the following day. Store in an airtight container to keep them fresh.

# 8

For less mess and ease

# pipe your batter

into the cases with a non-slip piping bag.

# 9

Sprinkle your iced cupcakes with

**sugar glitter for a touch of glamour.**

# 10

For an

# alternative English Cream Tea,

cut your cupcake in half and add strawberry jam and cream, top with a dab of cream and half a fresh strawberry.

# 11

A marriage made in

# cupcake heaven:

carrot cake cupcakes topped with cream cheese frosting and a few shavings of orange zest to decorate.

# 12

# Silicone cases are great for home baking

– no throw away paper cases and no crumbs!

# 13

Always **fill your paper cases in their baking trays,** if they are filled elsewhere it will be very difficult to move them.

# 14

If you are using honey, golden syrup
or treacle in your recipe,

**a little oil brushed on to your measuring spoon** will stop the liquid sticking.

# 15

# Every oven is different

and the recipe temperature is only a guide – sorry it's trial and error!

# 16

Hold your cupcakes

**on their base**

when decorating, as this is their

**strongest point.**

# 17

Cold ingredients can cause the mix
to contract and become tough –

**always have your eggs and butter at room temperature.**

# 18

Good quality cupcake cases are worth buying –

**thicker paper will hold its shape** during the baking process.

# 19

# Take care not to over-mix

as this makes the proteins in the flour stick together and prevents your cake batter from rising.

# 20

**Fold in** added ingredients such as chocolate pieces and nuts

**after the batter has been mixed**

– if you add them before the flour will stick to them, stopping them becoming part of the batter.

# 21

# Mouthwatering cupcakes

are dependent on using quality ingredients. They can only taste as good as the ingredients used!

# 22

The path to successful baking starts
with very accurate measures –

# invest in digital scales.

# 23

For a pretty topping for your
chocolate ganache cupcakes

**use a vegetable peeler to make chocolate curls**

by shaving the curls from the side of a bar.

# 24

Instead of the usual icing,

**top your lemon cupcakes with meringue** and pop them under the grill for a couple of minutes.

# 25

Use food colouring sparingly –

**use a toothpick to add gel or paste colouring**

– a little goes a long way!

# 26

Always use a **cupcake or muffin pan** to bake your cupcakes. This will ensure that your cakes will not spread outwards and **will fit snugly** into their cases.

# 27

If decorating with sugar beads or crystals

# add them immediately

onto soft frosting, if it begins to harden the decorations will simply roll off!

# 28

If you don't have a purpose-made cupcake box for transportation – pop them on a tray, and before you cover them, **stick toothpicks into the cupcakes** to prevent the cover touching them and ruining the frosting.

# 29

**For flat cupcakes**

bake at a slightly cooler temperature than usual –

**for peaked cakes** bake slightly higher.

# 30

Some mixture left over from making a large cake? Remember **most cake recipes can be used to bake cupcakes.**

# 31

# Cool cupcakes completely before frosting

or it could slip off!

# 32

Worried about additives in food colouring?

# Make your own colouring using fruit

such as raspberries or blueberries.

# 33

# Beware of using reduced fat margarine;

the fat content is not high enough to ensure good baking results.

# 34

**Sunlight will quickly fade sugar glitter and decorations**

– keep well away!

# 35

Cupcakes baked in silicone moulds will take slightly longer than usual as the

**silicone doesn't conduct heat as well as metal.**

# 36

Green tea and chocolate make
a wonderful flavoured sponge.

# Use powdered green tea powder called 'Matcha'

for making green tea frosting.

# 37

Transfer your cupcakes onto wire racks for cooling – if you lack space in your kitchen

**buy racks that can be stacked.**

# 38

# Cupcakes can be frozen un-iced for up to a month.

Allow them to defrost thoroughly in a cool place for 4–6 hours.

# 39

When filling your cases, try to **avoid spilling mixture around the edges,** as this can prevent your cakes rising evenly.

# 40

# Fancy a taste of chocolate heaven?

Pipe a generous swirl of chocolate butter cream on your cupcake and place a white chocolate rose in the centre. Sit back and watch them be devoured!

# 41

**If** you are **planning to freeze** your cupcakes – **use thicker paper cases** to make sure they keep their shape.

# 42

For a completely stunning look, buy special

**laser-cut decorative cupcake wrappers**

– these wrap around the paper case and are especially

**beautiful for weddings.**

# 43

Butter cream is naturally yellow –

**use white powdered food colouring** to lighten.

# 44

For a truly unique decoration have your own photos made into small round

**edible sugar images**

and place one on each of your iced cupcakes –

**lovely for a Christening!**

# 45

For a **simple but impressive gift,**

place one decorated cupcake in an individual clear cupcake box and tie with beautiful satin ribbon and a gift tag.

# 46

Make your own **bespoke cupcake stand**

by placing sugar paste iced cake boards one on top of another using cake pillars – trim the edges with ribbon.

# 47

For **an indulgent Valentine cupcake** – add some liqueur to your chocolate mix, decorate with rich velvety chocolate butter cream and top with a Champagne truffle!

# 48

If you are a novice,

**use butter cream icing**

it never sets completely hard
and so if you go wrong

**you can scrape it off**

and start again!

# 49

# The **secret to perfect butter cream:**

always sift your icing sugar and beat the mixture on high for at least 5 minutes.

# 50

Baking for a wedding or big party?

# Buy ready-made sugar decorations from online suppliers,

as they are often cheaper and available in larger quantities.

# Meg Avent

Through her work in cookery book publishing, Meg has commissioned some of the country's leading patisserie chefs. Inspired by their work, and having always had a passion for cake decorating, she went on to train at one of London's leading cake companies. She now runs her own business, Lemon Sky Cakes, specialising in unique and beautiful wedding and celebration cakes.

**www.lemonskycakes.co.uk**

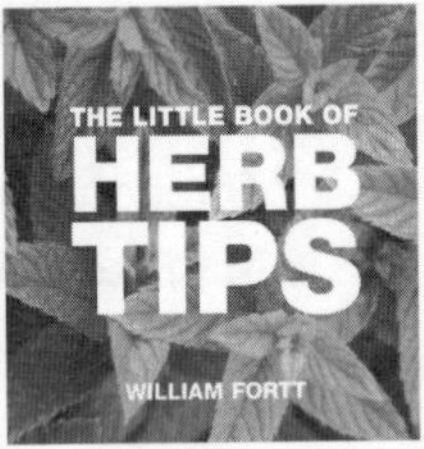

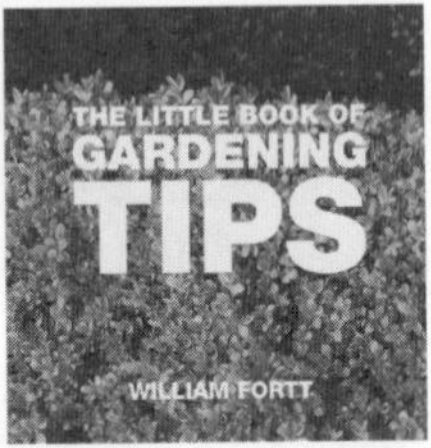

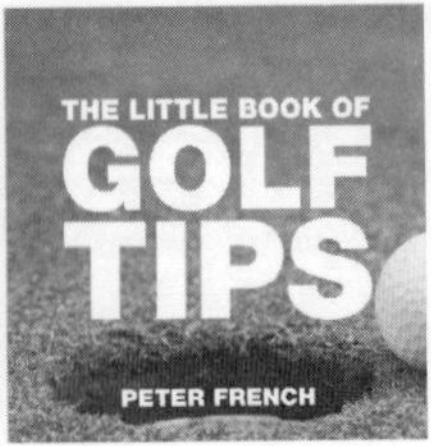


THE LITTLE BOOK OF

# TIPS SERIES

THE LITTLE BOOK OF
CHEESE
TIPS
ANDREW LANGLEY

THE LITTLE BOOK OF
WINE
TIPS
ANDREW LANGLEY

THE LITTLE BOOK OF
AGA
TIPS 2
RICHARD MAGGS

THE LITTLE BOOK OF
COFFEE
TIPS
ANDREW LANGLEY

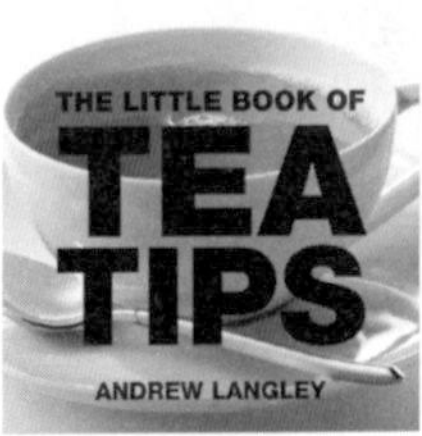
THE LITTLE BOOK OF
TEA
TIPS
ANDREW LANGLEY

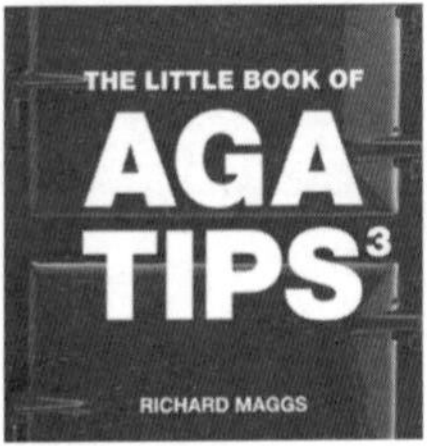
THE LITTLE BOOK OF
AGA
TIPS 3
RICHARD MAGGS

THE LITTLE BOOK OF
AGA
TIPS
RICHARD MAGGS

THE LITTLE BOOK OF
CHRISTMAS
AGA
TIPS
RICHARD MAGGS

THE LITTLE BOOK OF
RAYBURN
TIPS
RICHARD MAGGS

THE LITTLE BOOK OF
BRIDGE
TIPS
PETER FRENCH

THE LITTLE BOOK OF
CHESS
TIPS
PETER FRENCH

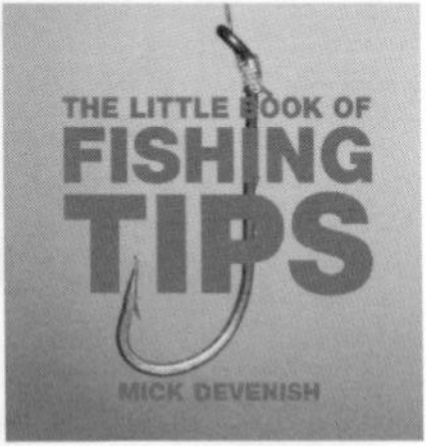
THE LITTLE BOOK OF
FISHING
TIPS
MICK DEVENISH

THE LITTLE BOOK OF
GREEN
TIPS
WILLIAM FORTT

THE LITTLE BOOK OF
KITTEN
TIPS
ANDREW LANGLEY

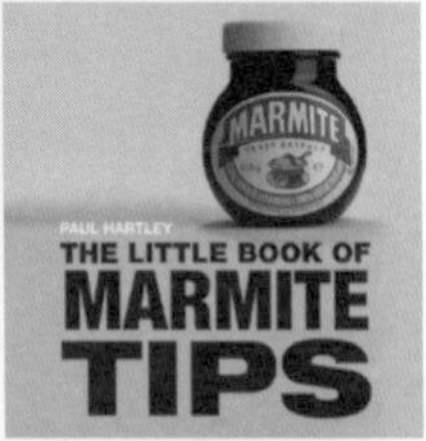
MARMITE
PAUL HARTLEY
THE LITTLE BOOK OF
MARMITE
TIPS

THE LITTLE BOOK OF
PUPPY
TIPS
ANDREW LANGLEY

THE LITTLE BOOK OF
WHISKY
TIPS
ANDREW LANGLEY

THE LITTLE BOOK OF
TRAVEL
TIPS
MEGAN DEVENISH

# Little Books of Tips from Absolute Press

Aga Tips
Aga Tips 2
Aga Tips 3
Christmas Aga Tips
Rayburn Tips
Tea Tips
Coffee Tips
Wine Tips
Whisky Tips
Beer Tips
Cocktail Tips
Cheese Tips
Bread Tips
Herb Tips
Spice Tips
Curry Tips
Marmite Tips
Olive Oil Tips
Vinegar Tips
Pasta Tips
Cupcake Tips
Cake Decorating Tips
Macaroon Tips
Chocolate Tips
Ice Cream Tips
Chefs' Tips
Barbecue Tips
Gardening Tips
Houseplant Tips
Golf Tips
Travel Tips
Fishing Tips
Green Tips
Frugal Tips
Poker Tips
Bridge Tips
Chess Tips
Backgammon Tips
Scrabble Tips
Puppy Tips
Kitten Tips